MW00915351

This book belongs to:

______________________________

(K) 2035-10

$30

22

23

$45

(L) 5e5

(T) 155